A big k

GW01454518

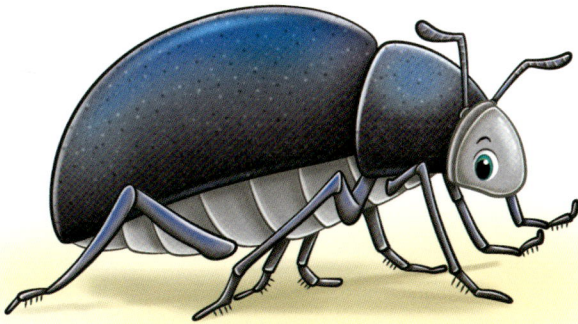

A big bug is
on the bun.

4

It is on the mug.

It is on the pot.

It is in the pan.

The bug sits
on the bin lid.

It is on the fan.

The fan gets rid of the bug.

# Before reading

**Say the sounds:** g o b h e r f u l

Ensure the children use the pure sounds for the consonants without the added "uh" sound, e.g. "llll" not "luh".

**Practise blending the sounds:** pot  mug  bug  lid  fan  bin  rid  sits  pan  bun  gets

**High-frequency words:** big  on  it  in   **Tricky words:** is  the  of

**Vocabulary check:** bug – What kind of creature is a bug? (usually a small insect) rid – What does it mean to "get rid of something"? (to remove something or throw it away)

**Story discussion:** What does the cover tell us about this story?

**Teaching points:** Children need to practise recognising and saying the word "of" as the sound represented for "f" is /v/.

# After reading

**Comprehension:**

- What were some of the things that the big bug was on?
- Who was watching the big bug?
- How did Sid get rid of the big bug?

**Fluency:** Speed read the words again from the inside front cover.